MW01240594

This Notebook Belongs To:

....

Published by Windmill Bay Books
WindmillBayBooks.com

Made in the USA
Middletown, DE
10 May 2023

30381405R00057